Locating and Preventing a Foreclosure, a Realtor's Guide

Locating and Preventing a Foreclosure, a Realtor's Guide

Cara L. Milgate

ISBN 978-1-304-43795-2

Table of Contents

San Francisco Bay Area Counties

(Alameda, Contra Costa, Marin, Napa, San Francisco, San Mateo, Santa Clara, Solano, Sonoma)

Did you know that most sale dates are listed on line "internet" for the public to view? You can locate opening bids, sale date exact time and day. You can view postponements and also the day of the sale the posting site will reflect, if foreclosed on whether the house went back to the bank or sold to a third party.

<u>Who is the Trustee?</u>

- The trustee is the company that the lender/servicer has retained to sell the home through a non-judicial foreclosure proceeding. The trustee will issue a trustee sale number (TS #) for each property when the properties transfer to a "foreclosure" status. The trustee sale number can be found on the recorded Notice of Default (NOD) and the Sale Date Notice. Both of these documents are recorded at the county recorder in which the property is located. These documents are public record. I have listed the addresses below of county recorder's offices within this publication.

- The Trustee is responsible for issuing a notice of default and all other legal requirements during the foreclosure process. The lender/servicer will instruct the trustee of the opening bid, postponing the sale and moving forward with the sale, etc.

What is the difference between a Posting Site and the Trustee Site!

Although many Trustee's manage their own on-line posting sites, some trustees outsource this responsibility to a third party "on-line posting site". Foreclosure posting site companies will have an "On-Line Presence" and/or a "Sale Hot Line".

What is a Trustee Sale Number?

When properties move into foreclosure the lender assigns the property to the trustee. The trustee then assigns a "Trustee Sale Number". This number is unique and will stay with the property throughout the foreclosure process. Once you have located this number, keep it in a safe location so you can reference it. This is the identification number to look up the property, once you have this number you only need to locate the Trustee Posting Site.

Special Note: if you see a TS number that looks like this "10-0232033". There is a very good chance the lender is Bank of America and the Trustee is ReconTrust. You must put a "20" in front of the TS number before entering in on the ReconTrust portal. So for example you would enter "2010-0232033"

What is a Notice of Default (NOD)?

This is a recorded document used in a non-judicial foreclosure process in California. This notice is sent to the homeowner and recorded at the county recorder of the location of the property. There is a 90 day default period (quiet period) beginning at time and date of recording. The lender and Trustee are not allowed to schedule a sale date on the property until the 90 day period has elapsed. The NOD will have the Trustee Name, Phone, Trustee Sale Number and many times the posting website for the foreclosure.

What is a Sale Date Notice?

After the 90 day period has elapsed after recording the Notice of Default, the lender/servicer has the legal right to issue a "Sale Date Notice". The lender must wait a minimum of 21 days before they can hold the auction on the property from the expiration date of the NOD. This notice is recorded at the county recorder of the location of the property. The notice should be taped to the door. The Sale Date Notice will have the Trustee Name, Phone Number, Trustee number and many times the posting website for the foreclosure. It will state the exact date, time and location of auction information. Please do not assume that because you did not receive this document that you do not have a sale date. If 90 days has elapsed from the NOD recording date you should be contacting the Trustee weekly to obtain confirmation that there is no sale date. The lender is not obligated to send this document certified. The sale will also be posted in the local newspaper.

What is a Parcel Number (APN)?

The Parcel Number (referred to as the APN) is a unique number assigned to each property by the county tax assessor of the county the property resides in. If you do not have a TS number and all you have is a property address, attempting to obtain the APN number is the first place to start. It can be found on-line by up the property taxes on any property at the County Assessors on-line website (which I have provided the links within this publication). Most all County Assessors have an on-line presence to look up property taxes, and when you locate the property tax information, you locate the APN number!

All you need to get started is a property address. From there you can start your investigation to gather as much information as possible. Obtaining any or all of the below information will assist you in locating the foreclosure information on line.

(1) Trustee Sale Number (TS #)

(2) Trustee Name, Contact Information

(3) Parcel Number (APN)

(4) Actual Sale date

- **If you already have the Trustee Sale Number (TS #), but you do not have the NOD or Sale Date Notice, proceed to the Trustee Posting Site Information in the following pages and attempt to locate the sale by trial and error.**

- **If you have the NOD or Sale Date Notice, please obtain the TS #, Trustee name and contact information on the document and proceed to the Trustee Information Page.**

Posting Sites Only

LPS

https://www.lpsasap.com/

Important: You must set up an account with LPS, this is free and you will have your own login and password

Automated Sales Line: 714.730.2727,
California Office: 714.247.7500,
Toll Free: 800.683.2468

Priority Posting

http://www.priorityposting.com/Priority/

Important: No Login Necessary

California Headquarters: Phone 800.570.3500,
Fax 800.570.3515

California Field Office: Phone 800.570.3500,
Fax 800.570.3515

RSVP (Residential Service Validated Publications)

http://www.rsvpforeclosures.com/ActivePages/NonSecure
Pages/PropertySearch.aspx

Important: No Login Necessary

Sale Hot Line: 877.778.7237,
Main: 925.603.8439,
Fax: 877.384.9861

USA-Foreclosure.com, LLC

http://www.usa-foreclosure.com/UserAccounts/userLogin.aspx

Important: No Login Necessary

Email: info@usa-foreclosure.com

TAC (Trustee Assistance Corporation)

www.tacforeclosures.com/sales/newdisclaimer.aspx

Important: No Login Necessary

Trustee

Cal Western Reconveyance

www.rppsales.com

Important: No Login Necessary

Tel: 619.590.1400, Toll Free: 800.566.6223, Automated Sales Line: 619.590.1221

Fax: 619.590.1496, Toll Free Fax: 800.310.2446, Email contact: info@rppsales.com

ReconTrust

http://www.recontrustco.com/upcoming_sales.aspx **(Trustee and Posting Site)**

Important: ReconTrust primarily processes Bank of America Foreclosures

Important: No Login Necessary

Tel: 800.281.8219

NDSC (National Default Servicing Corporations)

http://www.ndscorp.com/FsSales/PendingSales.aspx

Important: No Login Necessary

Tel: 602.264.6101

Fax: 602.264.6209

Quality Loan Service Corp.

www.qualityloan.com

Important: Please refer to LPS and Priority Posting for posting sites.

Tel: 877.886.9757

AUCTION.COM

www.auction.com, Tel: 800.793.6107

IF YOU DO NOT HAVE THE TS# NUMBER "START HERE"

- Before you do anything, type in the property address into the internet browser line with "Google". You would be surprised how much information comes up. You could get lucky and locate all the information you need just by performing this one search.

Obtain Parcel Number (APN)

(YOU MUST HAVE THE PROERTY ADDRESS)

Property Tax - Assessor Records California

Alameda County Assessor Records

www.acgov.org/MS/prop/index.aspx

Contra Costa County Assessor Records, CA

https://taxcolp.co.contra-costa.ca.us/taxpaymentrev3/summary/account_lookup.jsp

Marin County Assessor Records, CA

http://www.co.marin.ca.us/depts/AR/compass/index.asp

Napa County Assessor Records, CA

http://www.countyofnapa.org/assessorparceldata/

San Francisco County Assessor Records, CA

https://gate.link2gov.com/sfpropertytax/PropertySearch.aspx?TaxType=Secured

San Mateo County Assessor Records, CA

http://www.sanmateocountytaxcollector.org/SMCWPS/pages/secureSearch.jsp

Santa Clara County Assessor Records, CA

http://payments.scctax.org/payment/jsp/currentSecured.jsp

Solano County Assessor Records, CA

http://www.co.solano.ca.us/depts/ar/viewpropertyinfo.asp

Sonoma County Assessor Records, CA

http://www.sonoma-county.org/tax/proptax_pay.htm

If you are successful obtaining the parcel number, go back to the trustee posting sites and attempt to locate the property in this order:

- **LPS**
- **Priority Posting**
- **ReconTrust**
- **TAC**
- **If not listed above you will then have to locate property by trial and error, attempting the other trustee websites**
- **I will allow one free search per reader for the posting site location and/or trouble shooting questions. Please email me at cara.milgate@gmail.com and allow 24 hour response time!**

- **If you cannot find the property then you must obtain public records and obtain a copy of the Notice of Default and/or Trustee Sale Date Notice (See next page)**

* If you would like documentation of a past foreclosure please go to www.findmyforeclosuredate.com

County Recorder to obtain copies of NOD's and Sale Date Notice (will include TS #)

You must go to the county recorder to obtain a copy of the NOD and/or Sale Date Notice!

Alameda County Clerk - Recorder
1106 Madison St., 1st Floor, Oakland, CA 94607
Phone: (510) 272-6362 or 888-280-7708
http://www.acgov.org/auditor/clerk/

Contra Costa County Clerk - Recorder
555 Escobar St. Martinez, CA 94553
Phone: (925) 335-7900
http://www.ccclerkrec.us/connect/site/

Marin County Recorder
3501 Civic Center Drive, Suite 232, San Rafael, CA 94903
Phone: 415-473-6092
http://www.co.marin.ca.us/depts/AR/Main/Recorder.cfm

Napa County Clerk – Recorder
Carithers Building
900 Coombs St., Room 116, Napa, CA 94559
Recorder Phone: (707) 253-4105 Clerk Phone: (707) 253-4247
http://www.countyofnapa.org/Recorder-Clerk/

City and County of San Francisco Assessor – Recorder
1 Dr. Carlton B. Goodlett Pl., Room 190, San Francisco, CA 94102
Phone: (415) 554-5596 Fax: (415) 554-7915
http://www.sfassessor.org/index.aspx?page=77

San Mateo County Recorder
555 County Center, 1st Floor, Redwood City, CA 94063
Phone: (650) 363-4500 Fax: (650) 363-4843
http://www.smcare.org/recorder/default.asp

Santa Clara County Clerk – Recorder
70 West Hedding St., East Wing, 1st Floor, San Jose, CA 95110
Phone: 408-299-5688
http://www.sccgov.org/portal/site/rec/

Solano County Recorder
675 Texas St., Suite 2700, Fairfield, CA 94533
Phone: (707) 784-6200
http://www.co.solano.ca.us/depts/ar/recorder/recording_section/recording_official
_documents.asp

Sonoma County Assessor
585 Fiscal Drive, Suite 103F, Santa Rosa, CA 95403
Phone: (707) 565-2651 Fax: (707) 565-3905
http://www.sonoma-county.org/recorder/searching.asp

Important information to remember when tracking a foreclosure sale date

- Just because a home is in foreclosure does not mean there is a sale date. Once the NOD is filed the property is in a foreclosure status. Remember, 90 days must elapse from the recording of the NOD prior to the trustee issuing a sale date notice. The sale date notice is not automatic after 90 days, and can be delayed for many reasons.

- The surest way to find out if there is a sale date on the property is to call the trustee directly.

- If you do call the trustee and speak to a live person, you may or may not be able to receive the desired information unless you are the homeowner. The trustee could require third party authorization to obtain information verbally. The information is public record but it is at the trustee's discretion if they decide to communicate the information with you, but it is worth a call directly.

- If the sale is listed as cancelled, this typically means that the trustee must reschedule a new sale date and post it to the property. It DOES NOT mean that the trustee has to reissue a new Notice of Default, and most likely the property will remain in a foreclosure status.

- Do not assume that because the lender states that the sale is on hold or suspended that the trustees will not sell the home. Be sure and contact the trustee and obtain this information directly from them.

- Trustee's and Lenders can be very discrete when it comes to the sale date information, but if you are determined enough you will locate the website where the information is listed and obtain the trustee name, contact information and Trustee Sale Number.

- If there is a rescission to the Notice of Default, the trustee closes the file. There are three main reasons why a property is removed from foreclosure:

  - The lender instructs the Trustee to rescind the Notice of Default

  - House forecloses

  - House closes in a short sale

California Homeowner Bill of Rights Signed into Law. This law was much needed and put into law on January 1, 2013. Many lenders are not abiding by this law. If a homeowner gets foreclosed on and the lender has violated this law, the homeowner could have cause of action against the lender. Homeowners are getting their homes back after foreclosure when this law is applicable and legal remedies are pursued.

Attorney General Kamala D. Harris announced that the Homeowner Bill of Rights, which will protect homeowners and borrowers during the mortgage and foreclosure process, was signed into law today by Governor Edmund G. Brown Jr.

The Homeowner Bill of Rights prohibits a series of inherently unfair bank practices that have needlessly forced thousands of Californians into foreclosure. The law restricts dual-track foreclosures, where a lender forecloses on a borrower despite being in discussions over a loan modification to save the home. It also guarantees struggling homeowners a single point of contact at their lender with knowledge of their loan and direct access to decision makers, and imposes civil penalties on fraudulently signed mortgage documents. In addition, homeowners may require loan servicers to document their right to foreclose. The laws will go into effect on January 1, 2013, and borrowers can access courts to enforce their rights under this legislation.

The Homeowner Bill of Rights builds upon and extends reforms first negotiated in the recent national mortgage settlement between 49 states and leading lenders. Attorney General Harris secured up to $18 billion for California homeowners in that agreement, and has also built a Mortgage Fraud Strike Force to investigate crime and fraud associated with mortgages and foreclosures.

"The California Homeowner Bill of Rights will give struggling homeowners a fighting shot to keep their home," said Attorney General Harris. "This legislation will make the mortgage and foreclosure process more fair and transparent, which will benefit homeowners, their community, and the housing market as a whole."

"Californians should not have to suffer the abusive tactics of those who would push foreclosure behind the back of an unsuspecting homeowner," said Governor Brown. "These new rules make the foreclosure process more transparent so that loan servicers cannot promise one thing while doing the exact opposite."

The Homeowner Bill of Rights consists of a series of related bills, including two identical bills that were passed on July 2 by the state Senate and Assembly: AB 278 (Eng, Feuer, Pérez, Mitchell) and SB 900 (Leno, Evans, Corbett, DeSaulnier, Pavley, Steinberg).

The California Homeowner Bill of Rights also contains a variety of bills outside of the conference committee process. These will enhance law enforcement responses to mortgage and foreclosure-related crime, in part by empowering the Attorney General to call a grand jury in response to financial crimes spanning multiple jurisdictions. Additional elements will help communities fight blight related to foreclosure, and provide enhanced protections for tenants in foreclosed homes. Please see the attached fact sheet for the status of these bills.

The California Homeowner Bill of Rights was introduced February 29, 2012 at a press conference featuring Assembly Speaker John A. Pérez and Senate President pro Tem Darrell Steinberg and bill authors from the Assembly and Senate.

California Foreclosure (Non-Judicial State) Time Line

The borrower (Trustor) is in default after the 1st payment is missed, but in practical terms, most Lenders (Beneficiaries) do not begin the process until the third payment is missed. If the Lender cannot resolve the defaulted payment amount with the borrower through Modification or other solutions, the Lender will retain a trustee to begin Foreclosure proceedings. Much correspondence from the bank will come prior to this, acceleration notices which will have deadlines on them to pay the account current, etc.

Day 1
Missed Payment: It's the first of the month (30 full days have gone by since due date), and the mortgage payment is due. The borrower misses a payment.

Day 31
Second Missed Payment: It's the first of the month, and the borrower misses a second payment.

Day 32

Default: The borrower is in default the second day after the second missed mortgage payment is due.

Day 40-90

Notice of Default (NOD): Some time in the next 60 days, the borrower will receive a letter stating that the Notice of Default (NOD) has been recorded. The date of the NOD depends on the ender.

Day 130-180

Silent Period: After the NOD is recorded there is a 90 day silent period in which borrower may pay all back payments and fees to cure the default. After the silent period, the lender sends the borrower a letter setting the date of the Trustee's Sale, typically three weeks after the end of the silent period. 5 days before Trustee's sale Right to Cure: The borrower may cure the default up to five days before the property is sold.

Day 150 - 200

Trustee's Sale: The house is sold at a foreclosure sale or auction.

Day 180 - 230

Eviction: The borrower has the right to remain in the house for up to 30 days after the house is sold.

Helpful Websites and Links

- **Fannie Mae Property Lookup:**
  http://loanlookup.fanniemae.com/loanlookup/
- **Freddie Mac Property Lookup:**
  https://ww3.freddiemac.com/corporate/
- **Am I eligible for a Home Affordable Modification? Answer these questions:**
  http://www.makinghomeaffordable.gov/modification_elig ibility.html
- **Estimate Property Value: www.redfin.com**
  IRS Insolvency Test
  o http://irsinsolvencytest.blogspot.com/
  Federal Debt Cancellation Relief
  o http://feddebtcancellation.blogspot.com/
  California Mortgage Forgiveness Debt Relief
  o http://califmtgforegiveness.blogspot.com/

Complaint Website Sites

https://www.federalreserveconsumerhelp.gov/consumercomplaint.cfm

www.helpwithmymortgage.gov

www.consumerfinance.gov

www.ftccomplaints.gov

www.naag.org/attorneys_general.php

www.consumeraction.gov/state.shtml

https://econsumer.ftccomplaintassistant.gov/

www.bbb.org

www.sigtarp.gov/pages/hotline.aspx

https://independentforeclosurereview.com/ **(foreclosure between Jan. 1, 2009 & Dec. 31, 2009)**

http://oag.ca.gov/consumers

For anyone who lost their home to foreclosure between January 1, 2008 and December 31, 2011 send email to: administrator@nationalmortgagesettlement.com for a cash settlement

California Purchase Money Loans, 1st, 2nd, 3rd, etc....

After Foreclosure!

Under _California CCP 580b_ the lender is barred from pursuing a deficiency judgment against you if the loan(s) is purchase money, which yours appear to be because you have not refinanced.

A non-recourse loan is a loan that the bank can only look to their secured interest. In other words, they can only foreclose; they cannot get a deficiency judgment and chase you into bankruptcy collecting it.

So how is a second or third (or more) mortgage a non-recourse loan? Simple, it was purchase money for your home. A purchase money loan is one where the money went from the lender, to escrow, and then to the seller or to pay purchase closing costs. In California purchase money loans made on your home (note: not second home or investment properties) are non-recourse.

California CCP 580b (It is the LAW)

No deficiency judgment shall lie in any event after a sale of real property or an estate for years therein for failure of the purchaser to complete his or her contract of sale, or under a deed of trust or mortgage given to the vendor to secure payment of the balance of the purchase price of that real property or estate for years therein, or under a deed of trust or mortgage on a dwelling for not more than four families given to a lender to secure repayment of a loan which was in fact used to pay all or part of the purchase Price of that dwelling occupied, entirely or in part, by the purchaser.

Where both a chattel mortgage and a deed of trust or mortgage have been given to secure payment of the balance of the combined purchase price of both real and personal property, no deficiency judgment shall lie at any time under any one thereof if no deficiency judgment would lie under the deed of trust or mortgage on the real property or estate for years therein.

Homeowner to Pay Delinquent Property Taxes on their home in Foreclosure!

Delinquent property taxes become a lien on the property. They will be wiped off after a foreclosure. When the foreclosure proceeds, the house will be sold for whatever the highest bid amount is. These proceeds will be used to pay off everything that is affecting the house. First to be paid is any delinquent or currently due property taxes. The county gets paid first and the ex-homeowner is no longer responsible as he/she are no longer owners of this property.

The same outcome regarding of a short sale in regards to real estate. Whoever is purchasing home will put in an offer on the house. The offer typically will include an estimate Hud 1 (closing statement) from the title/escrow company. This should include liens on the property (including delinquent or prorated property taxes due). It is up to the new buyer and lender to conduct their due diligence in regards to liens on the property to assure proper transfer of clean title to the new owner.

If a homeowner is desperately trying to save their home and are in foreclosure, they need to make wise decisions. Not everyone will be granted a loan modification. Therefore any monies the homeowner pays out towards a home in which they do not know if they will own will be lost. We highly suggest that homeowners get proper counseling and advice when making these decisions. Homeowners need to consider all options, and one important aspect is the ability to have enough savings to transition into new housing if there is not a favorable resolution to the homeowner keeping his/her property.

Lenders Cannot Require Real Estate Agents to Reduce Their Commission on a Short Sale

Civil Code 580(e)

If a lender is requiring you to reduce your commission, please send executive complaint to the lender utilizing the information and statue below. If you do not speak up you may lose the opportunity to retain your full commission!

The California Legislature placed limits upon a lender's ability to condition a short sale approval. California Code of Civil Procedure section 580e(d) **prohibits a lender from requiring the seller to pay additional compensation to a lender in order to obtain the lenders' approval of the short sale**: (b) A holder of a note shall not require the trustor, mortgagor, or maker of the note to pay any additional compensation, aside from the proceeds of the sale, in exchange for the written consent to the sale, and (e) Any purported waiver (by borrower) [...] shall be void and against public policy.

Same law for reducing commission:

The demand that the seller breaches the listing agreement and require a reduced commission in order to increase the money paid to a lender is expressly prohibited by this statute.

California tort law provides the real estate broker with a civil cause of action for intentional interference with contract against a lender that induces a seller to breach a written listing agreement. *Dryden v. Tri-Valley Growers*, 65 Cal.App.3d 990, 995.

Real Estate Agents also have a claim for Unfair Business Practices. California Business & Professions Code section 17200 et seq., California's unfair competition law, prohibits any unlawful, unfair, or fraudulent business act or practice. Cal. Bus. & Prof. Code § 17200. The "act or practice" aspect of section 17200 covers any single act of misconduct, as well as ongoing misconduct. *See Klein v. Earth Elements, Inc.* (1997) 59 Cal.App.4th 965, 969 n.3. To state a claim under section 17200, a plaintiff must only establish that the act or practice is either unlawful or unfair. *Albillo v. Intermodal Container Services, Inc.* (2003) 114 Cal.App.4th 190, 206. Here, (*lender's name*) condition that the agents reduce their commission in order to obtain (*lender's name*) approval of the short sale is unlawful under California Code of Civil Procedure section 580e. The practice is also unfair because it encourages sellers of real property to breach written listing agreement with licensed real estate brokers.

This letter informs the Lender that its effort to condition a short sale approval on a reduction of realtor's commission is both unlawful and tortuous under California law.

Deficiency Judgment Law Passes

Great News for California Distressed Homeowners
Prohibit of Deficiency Judgment of 1st Loans
SB931 Passes on January 1st, 2011

Senate Bill 931 (SB 931) pertaining to California Short Sale Deficiencies was signed by the Governor on September 30th. Beginning January 1st, 2011 any first mortgages that accept a short sale will not be able to obtain a deficiency judgment against a seller after the completion of a short sale. If a lender provides written consent to a short sale on a first mortgage, the lender must accept the sales proceeds as full payment and discharge the remaining balance due on the loan. The new law will apply to all first mortgage loans secured by one to four residential units, including purchase money, hard money and refinanced loans. The new law does not prevent the lender from seeking damages for fraud or waste by the borrower.

The legislative counsel's summary of the bill follows:

"This bill would prohibit a deficiency judgment under a note secured by a first deed of trust or first mortgage for a dwelling of not more than 4 units in any case in which the (owner) sells the dwelling for less than the remaining amount of the indebtedness due at the time of sale with the written consent of the holder of the first deed of trust or first mortgage. The bill would provide that written consent of the holder of the first deed of trust or first mortgage to that sale shall obligate that holder to accept the sale proceeds as full payment and to fully discharge the remaining amount of the indebtedness on the first deed of trust or first mortgage. "

The new law only applies to mortgages in the first lien position. It is very important for any borrowers with a second lien to get in writing that future deficiency rights are waived. While many attorneys believe that if a second mortgage is purchase money, that the seller will be protected under the non-recourse laws, there has not been any definitive case law to reflect this.

Homeowners should avoid forensic loan audits

The scheme cheats homeowners to pay up-front fees for a forensic review of their lender's practices, but are provided no actual foreclosure relief. Homeowners are encouraged to pay for an audit of their mortgage loan file to determine their lender's compliance with state and federal mortgage-lending laws. This audit is a misleading claim offered to homeowners as an instrument they can use to gain ground and speed up the loan-modification procedure.

Those who offer forensic loan audits use inflated and misleading claims to persuade homeowners to pay up-front fees for services that produce no actual foreclosure relief.

Homeowners are encouraged to pay for an audit of their mortgage loan file to determine their lender's compliance with state and federal mortgage-lending laws. This audit is pitched to homeowners as a tool they can use to gain leverage and speed up the loan-modification process.

In truth, there is no evidence or statistical data to support claims that forensic loan audits -- even if performed by a licensed, legitimate and trained auditor, mortgage professional or lawyer -- will help homeowners get loan modifications or provide any other foreclosure relief. Nonetheless, evidence or statistical data will not help homeowners obtain loan modifications or provide any other foreclosure relief, even if they were performed by licensed auditors.

Lenders are not reacting to the forensic audits; there really is no need to.

The forensic audit is best suited as a pre-litigation tool and unless the homeowners are willing to fund $10,000-$20,000 law suit against their bank, the forensic audit appears useless.

Homeowners should ask for examples of clients they have helped and testimonials. In regards to what is most effective in the foreclosure crisis, the companies that can provide solid evidence of homeowners they have successfully provided service too, should be the only assistance the homeowner should consider in trusting their homes.

IRS Insolvency Test

Mortgage Forgiveness Income Tax

Millions of people are afraid they will owe income tax on phantom income that results when they either lose their house in foreclosure, or when they do a short sale.

This article explains why you probably have nothing to worry about, at least as far as the IRS is concerned. As always you need to get tax advice only from your own qualified tax advisor.

Let's start with the simple fact that when you borrow money, the money you borrow is not income. You have to pay it back. So whatever you charge on a credit card, or whatever you borrow on a mortgage, is borrowed money that must get paid back. Not income. Clear? Good.

Now, let's continue and say that you borrow money and then the lender says "no, you aren't going to pay this back."

Now that money you borrowed is no longer owed. So it becomes, in the government's eyes, income to you.

And you owe income tax on income, right?

So a lot of folks have stressed out and worried that they owe income tax on the amount of their mortgage that they didn't pay. Let's use an example.

If your mortgage was $300,000 but you did a short sale for $200,000, then you have $100,000 in income that the IRS calls cancellation of indebtedness income.

If your tax rate is 30%, you would owe $30,000 on top of having this awful foreclosure or short sale on your credit report.

However, the way the law has read, there are two exceptions. One exception says that if you are insolvent at the time you get this cancellation of indebtedness income, then you owe no tax.

What does insolvent mean? It means if you add up all your assets such as cash and the value of your house (but excluding many retirement funds), and you subtract all your liabilities such as your mortgage and the amount you owe on your other loans, then you end up with a negative number. You owe more than you have. You are technically insolvent.

So you have no tax liability.

Also, if the mortgage is non-recourse, then you have no tax liability. So for many states such as California, loans used to purchase a primary residence are non-recourse and therefore, for these purchase money mortgages, there is no liability for cancellation of debt.

And there is now a new law that Congress passed and President George W. Bush just signed, H.R. 3648, The Mortgage Forgiveness Debt Relief Act of 2007. That Act says two things. First, that the insolvency test is no longer the only test that says whether or not you have cancellation of debt income tax liability.

Now, you do not have cancellation of debt income tax liability if do a short sale or a foreclosure, so long as the house is your principal residence and the amount of cancellation of debt does not exceed $2 million.

For investors, the insolvency loophole will continue to be critical because they may have houses and properties that they lose in foreclosure and because they are insolvent, they can avoid federal tax liability for cancellation of indebtedness.

This law is welcome but will not have much affect because most people already could escape federal tax liability based upon the insolvency test. And it does not affect investment property. However, every little bit helps.

This is not intended as tax advice, please see your CPA for your specific situation.

SB458 A LAW THAT HELPS THE HOUSING CRISIS

Gov. Jerry Brown on signing SB 458 into law. SB 458 extends the protections of SB 931 (2010), to ensure that any lender that agrees to a SHORT SALE MUST ACCEPT THE AGREED UPON SHORT SALE PAYMENT AS PAYMENT IN FULL OF THE OUTSTANDING BALANCE OF ALL LOANS.

Under previous law a first mortgage holder could accept an agreed-upon short sale payment as full payment for the outstanding balance of the loan, but unfortunately, the rule did not apply to junior lien holders. SB 458 extends the protections of SB 931 to junior liens.

Once a lender has agreed to accept a short sale payment on a property, all lien holders – those in first position and in junior positions – will consider the outstanding balance as paid in full and the homeowner will not be held responsible for any additional payments on the property. It is effective NOW. (CCP §580e)

Civil Code Section 2923.6

(a) The Legislature finds and declares that any duty servicers may have to maximize net present value under their pooling and servicing agreements is owed to all parties in a loan pool, or to all investors under a pooling and servicing agreement, not to any particular party in the loan pool or investor under a polling and servicing agreement, and that a servicer acts in the best interests of all parties to the loan pool or investors in the pooling and servicing agreement if it agrees to or implements a loan modification or workout plan for which both of the following apply:

   (1) The loan is in payment default, or payment default is reasonably foreseeable.

   (2) Anticipated recovery under the loan modification or workout plan exceeds the anticipated recovery through foreclosure on a net present value basis.

(b) It is the intent of the Legislature that the mortgagee, beneficiary, or authorized agent offers the borrower a loan modification or workout plan if such a modification or plan is consistent with its contractual or other authority.

(c) This section shall remain in effect only until January 1,2013, and as of that date is repealed, unless a later enacted statute, that is enacted before January 1, 2013, deletes or extends that date.

Hanging on to Properties that have Negative Equity!

Why do homeowners insist on hanging on to their homes when they are hundreds of thousands of dollars upside down in their equity? I have met with thousands of homeowners during my career. In the past two years most of the homeowners I have spoke to are desperately fighting to save their homes from foreclosure. I ask important questions right away: (a) how long have you owned your home? (b) How much of your own money have you put into this home? (c) Ideally how long would you like to live in this home? (d) How much of a factor is the area and schools in regards to your children (if applicable)? (e) How much of a monthly payment can you afford? And many more questions that are relevant to what the homeowner deems important factors.

I find that most times if a client is trying to hang on to a home that is $100,000+ negative equity they are "emotionally attached" to their home. It is human nature that when someone is trying to take something away from us we try to hang on even tighter and lose all reasoning and perspective. I listen, take notes and give clients valid options based on actual experience of past and current clients.

There are many valid reasons why negative equity is not an issue for homeowners and obtaining an affordable monthly payment is the only and/or main factor: (a) A homeowner has to live somewhere, if they lose their home they will have to pay rent (b) Many times a modification can obtain payments as low if not lower than current market rent (c) As a homeowner you have interest you can write off on your tax returns, as a renter there is very little tax advantage (d) Because of credit history and/or income levels homeowners might have a difficulty ever buying a home again or in any type of near future (e) The embarrassment of losing their home (neighbors, family, friends, co-workers, etc) (f) And possibly one of the most important reasons is uprooting their children from the home, school and neighborhood.

Go for the Modification first, allows 3-12 months and hopefully you will get what you are looking for. There are choices out there, but you have to obtain experience and professional assistance.

www.ingramcontent.com/pod-product-compliance
Lightning Source LLC
Chambersburg PA
CBHW030011190526
45157CB00015B/2310